THO~~UGH~~
PR
HEA

Lionel Fanthorpe

BISHOPSGATE PRESS

This book is dedicated to a quartet of "dear and beloved physicians", Drs. Eric and Margaret Payne, Nick Jones and my son-in-law Iain Jarvis, together with my equally 'dear and beloved' daughter, medical physicist Stephanie.

© 1995 Lionel Fanthorpe

ISBN: 1 85219 067 1

British Library Cataloguing in Publication Data
Fanthorpe, Lionel
Thoughts and prayers for healing times
1. Christian life. Prayers - Devotional works.

All enquiries and requests relevant to this title should be sent to the publisher, Bishopsgate Press Ltd., Bartholomew House, 15 Tonbridge Road, Hildenborough, Kent TN11 9BH.

Printed by Whitstable Litho Printers Ltd., Millstrood Road, Whitstable, Kent

Contents

Foreword

by Canon Stanley Mogford, M.A.

If any one wish could be ours for the asking, and granted, what would it be? Most of us would almost certainly ask for wealth. It must be Heavenly to be free of all debts and never again experience poverty. Others, better blessed financially, might well choose Power. They know they would enjoy arranging and dominating the lives of all around them. The majority of us, with wiser heads, and more mature in age, would go without hesitation for Good Health.

Izaak Walton, in his *Compleat Angler* would be speaking for many of us:-- *Look to your Health and if you have it praise God and value it.*

Good Health is surely God's Will for us all. We long for it for our children; He will surely equally long for it for all His. Sadly it has to be faced that not all of them have it. Some struggle with ill health, and consequent pain, all their lives and have long periods in hospital. Others have intermittent bouts of ill health and are never sure when such attacks will overtake them. The older of us will come to experience with advancing age, the stiffening of joints, failing senses, and the imperfections of an ageing memory. Good Health may be our wish. Ill Health may be our Reality.

The Reverend Lionel Fanthorpe has written this small book for all those who have had to face pain and suffering and in particular for those who spend long and sometimes anxious times in hospital. If he could he would be by their bedside in person. As he cannot he has sought to comfort and strengthen them through his pen.

The irony of it is that this book comes from a man who is blessed with almost miraculous good health. He is a grandfather so not all that young. He swims every day. He lifts weights and teaches Judo. Retired from full-time teaching he now lectures, preaches and tutors almost non-stop. He is the author of well over 200 books. Where there is so much energy and vitality and all round good health one might expect to find only the barest understanding of the narrowness, the restrictions, the self absorption of the world of the sick and disabled.

The book proves him otherwise. He appears in every page of it to "counsel with sensitivity, with gentleness, with compassion, with understanding." It will prove a rich source of comfort and strength to all who read it.

Canon Stanley Mogford, M.A.
Cardiff

Introduction

The Bible contains many accounts of those who suffered sickness and injury, but who found healing and new strength to cope with their problems.

There is the Genesis account of Jacob's wrestling with the Angel at Bethel. That experience left him with a permanent limp. What meaning can we extract today from Jacob's long and arduous conflict there? He exerted himself beyond his mortal strength, beyond the limits of human endurance. His heart and mind were set upon obtaining the blessing that he longed for.

Some illness and injury may come upon us in similar ways today. There are many good men and women who burn themselves out in their single-minded pursuit of some great and good cause. That is their choice and their right. If we choose to wrestle like Jacob in order to attain some great goal, we too may run the risk of having to pay for it later.

Saint Paul had a 'thorn in the flesh'. A close reading of the Acts and Epistles suggests that he may have had difficulty with his vision. He certainly suffered a great deal of pain and discomfort during his tireless missionary work, which brings us to another vitally important consideration.

It is sometimes tempting to think, and to say, that illness or injury seems unjust, unfair and unmerited. A medical missionary may be taken ill while tending the sick. An unselfish rescuer may be drowned, or burned, while gallantly attempting to save others. A Christian speaker can be killed or injured in an accident while on the way to a meeting to proclaim the word of God. It does not seem to make sense, and yet it happens. Why?

In a rational Universe of cause and effect, a mechanical fault in a car or plane will - like the Tower of Siloam - injure the good, the bad, and all those who lie somewhere between. A virus or bacterium will be inhaled, ingested, or will make its insidious way into the victim through a cut, or graze, irrespective of whether the person is on his, or her, way to commit a crime, to visit the sick, or to lead worship. The body which is well fed, regularly exercised, and properly rested and relaxed will have far higher resistance to illness and much faster recovery from injury than the body which is abused, over-stressed, under-nourished or desperate for more rest. The old Biblical wisdom of resting on the seventh day was never intended as a negative prohibition but as a glorious and golden opportunity for essential rest and recuperation, for that recharging of our physical, mental and spiritual batteries which the body, mind and spirit need. It is a vital part of the Maker's Instructions.

But accepting the consistency, the rationality, the logic and reason of our universe does not preclude the wonderful and the miraculous. Life is, in fact, an ever-changing kaleidoscope of the miraculous, the mysterious and the mundane. Because there are general and well understood causes and effects, stimuli and responses, it does not mean that exceptions cannot exist: they do. Our Lord's own miracles are very well attested and undoubtedly took place exactly as the Gospel writers describe them. The blind were able to see again; the lame could walk; the paralysed recovered the use of their limbs; the deaf were able to hear and the dumb were able to speak. Christ raised Lazarus from the dead, and went on to rise from the tomb Himself, triumphant and eternal on the first Easter morning. He fed five thousand with a handful of loaves and fishes. He stilled the storm. He stood and talked with Moses and Elijah on the Mount of Transfiguration. Christ's work is *fact*. It is a vitally important part of history, as real as the Battle of Hastings, the signing of Magna Carta and the coronation of Queen Elizabeth II, and it is infinitely more important.

Whatever the sickness, whatever the injury, whatever pessimistic prognosis may come from orthodox medicine, miracles of healing, recovery and restoration still occur. We can assist and encourage them by faith, by prayer, by courage, by hope, and by developing an unconquerable will. Just when and why miracles occur are quintessential parts of the central mystery of the universe. Christ Himself taught us that faith is the golden key which unlocks the mystery and that if we have faith the size of a mustard seed, it is enough to move the mountains of despair and weakness, discomfort and pain.

God made you. God loves you. It is no part of His will that you should be sick or injured. He wants your health and happiness even more than you and your loved ones do. Let your faith, hope and courage work in harmony with the skill and care of doctors, nurses and carers so that through medicine, or miracle, or both, God's will of love and healing may be made perfect in you.

Making the Best of Things

George Borrow's Gypsy always knew that whatever was *not* there to enjoy, there would still be the wind on the heath for him. Our responsibility in life is to ensure that our consciousness, our moods, attitudes and decision making powers are all centred on this present moment. The task that our God has given us is to take hold of *now*. The past has gone beyond our reach; the future is still in His hands. The ship that we're steering is HMS NOW. In this case HMS stands for Help Me Steer! We must make the most of the instant. If sickness or injury has prevented us from making music ourselves, then let us listen to the music of others. We remember the words of C. S. Lewis in this connection: "When we have learned to love our neighbours as ourselves, we are then permitted to love ourselves as much as we love our neighbours." If we think about it in that way we can enjoy the activities of those around us as if those activities were our own. We can read a good book, watch an exciting television programme or video, see an Olympic athlete clearing a hurdle or winning a race and, in our minds, enter into that activity with him or her.

It is the sad, mean, and unworthy thought which fills us with envy and self-pity when we see a fit, whole, healthy person doing something which is beyond our present strength. We can escape from the prison of illness by truly caring more for others than for ourselves and in so doing we can, in a wonderful sense, live their lives with them despite our own physical challenges and disabilities.

There is always some worthwhile thing to think about. The loving Christian mind, though trapped in the frailest and weakest body, is still capable of constant prayer for others and for its own needs. There is no greater power than the power of prayer. Even in the last extremity, though nothing should remain to us but conscious thought itself -- if that thought is directed to God in prayer it is still a magnificently worthwhile thing to do.

Prayer

Lord of all strength, take pity on my weakness. Help me to make the best of things. Help me to use the power and strength that still remains in me for your service, and, if all I can do for others at this time is to pray for them, help me to pray for them effectively. Remind me that, especially when things seem to be at their lowest, You always hear my prayer. Amen.

Never Completely Helpless

It is one of the wonders of human life that, when sickness or injury prevents us from doing things for ourselves, God provides loving carers who will see to our needs and help us. The mind which has turned itself towards God is like an enormous continent turning towards the sun in the early morning. His strength is made perfect in our weakness. Our dependence upon families and friends, loving Christian brothers and sisters, nurses, doctors and physiotherapists, reminds us of our ultimate dependence upon God. It sometimes requires much greater strength of mind and character to allow others to do things for us than to want to be in control of the situation and to do things ourselves. We may be in a position where we no longer have the choice of which action to take, or what movement to make, but we do have the choice of how we will accept what is offered and what is done for us, and, in making that choice, we demonstrate by our courage and good humour that we are far from helpless.

Prayer

Lord of all strength, director and controller of the power that fires the stars and sets the limits of the galaxy, You were once content to be a helpless Babe in Mary's arms at Bethlehem. Help us to cope with our weakness and helplessness, and to accept what is done for us with patience, cheerfulness and gratitude. We ask it in the name of Christ our Lord. Amen.

A Thorn in the Flesh

A thorn in the flesh is not always discernible, even when it's a thorn in our own flesh. It is even harder for us to understand what others may be having to put up with. There is a North American Indian proverb which is well worth taking to heart: "Never judge a person until you have walked for a day in his, or her, moccasins." If I know about the chronic pain that my neighbour is bearing in silence, it will be easy for me to understand his, or her, impatience and irritability when I ask to borrow his lawnmower. If I know about the toothache, the migraine, or the pain in the arthritic joint that my friend at work is having to put up with all the time, it will help me to understand why he, or she, is not being as co-operative as I had hoped. And when things are the other way round, when it's my flesh that has the proverbial thorn in it, Lord, help me to overcome, help me to focus my attention on something else, something purposeful and positive, so that I can conquer the pain and discomfort of this particular thorn and get on with the important business of living and trying to do Your will.

Poem

"Father, forgive them," said the Lord
"They know not what they do."
Christ rose from the dark depths of pain
With His perspective true.
He thought of Mary and of John
And of the dying thief.
The needs of others -- not His own --
Caused all His tears and grief.
Defend us, Lord, from selfishness.
May all our pity turn
To others and their sharper thorns
As of their pain we learn.

Prayer

Lord give me the sensitivity and imagination to sympathise with others and to accept that they may be suffering from pain and discomfort of which I am unaware. When I myself have a problem, help me to mask it so that I can keep my suffering to myself and reserve my sympathy for those around me who really deserve it. I ask it in the Name of Christ who suffered and died for us and rose again triumphant. Amen.

Passing the Time

Shakespeare composed a very effective speech about the subjective nature of time: for some it runs, for some it walks, while for others it stands still. We might add that in the darkest, the dreariest and most boring of situations, it almost seems to go backwards. One of the longest nights I can ever remember was spent on the deck of a cross Channel ferry, when the sensations of seasickness were so intense that I thought the morning -- and the harbour -- would never come. Leaning precariously over the side, clinging grimly to the rail, looking at my watch every five minutes, I suspected the digits were going backwards as the hours stubbornly refused to pass.

By contrast there are all too brief and fleeting moments of exquisite and intense pleasure: a glimpse of brilliant constellations; playing with a tiny kitten and a strand of wool; standing breathless but triumphant on top of a mountain after a long, hard climb; watching an arrowhead of wild geese in flight; listening to a church organ producing harmonies as majestic and mysterious as those of the legendary lost chord. Those moments which we would like to last for ever are gone almost before we have time to experience them properly. Such is the subjective interaction between the phenomenon of time and the perceptive powers of the mind.

When we are ill or injured, time seems to drag very heavily indeed, and yet, because it is such a subjective thing, we can bring our wills to bear upon it. We can fill this slowly moving time with prayer for those we love, with contemplation of the glory and the wonder of God and the universe he has made for us to explore and enjoy. We can find interesting puzzles to solve, and interesting mind games to play. There are jigsaws (if we are able to use hand and eye); there are television programmes and video recordings to watch; there are radios and cassette tapes to which we can listen. And so, rather surprisingly, when we try hard to think positively about it, there is a real element of choice in this strange phenomenon of subjective time. Positive thinking and a strong will can make time our servant not our master. Interest and boredom are not moods which come upon us like predatory birds, devouring us as they choose. A strong and positive will dictates moods and not vice versa. When time is dragging, we can consciously and deliberately direct ourselves to be *interested*.

Prayer

Lord, you are the Master of all time and space, of every dimension, known and unknown. You have made us in Your image; help us to reflect Your image in our mastery of time. Teach us to be interested whatever our circumstances; help us to be positive and motivated wherever we are. Show us that the best possible thing to do with our time is to worship You, to contemplate Your wonders and to pray for others. We ask it in the Name of Christ our Lord. Amen.

The Problem of Pain

Of all the doubts and anxieties that assail the Christian mind this problem of pain and suffering is one of the very worst. We must ask ourselves (because above all our God and Father wants us to be honest) why an all-powerful and all-loving God permits the suffering and sorrow we see constantly in the world around us.

Innocent children are starving to death. We see the equally innocent victims of bombs, mines and shells, maimed, blinded and hideously scarred.

We cry out for answers.

But the answers are hard to find.

I cannot, I do not, and I will not doubt that God is absolute love and absolute power -- for Christ Himself told us so and He more than any other being knows the eternal truth above the Divine Nature.

There are two guide lines which may help us climb up out of this dark and terrible abyss. Our first thought is the vital importance of free will, without which there can be no true love. There can be no doubt -- from all our own personal, earthly experience and knowledge of life, and from all that Christ has taught us -- that love is the source of the greatest joy. Love is the greatest good in all our universes: physical, mental and spiritual. So then, if the very existence of love necessitates freedom of will, the grave risk of wrong choices and their evil consequences must also exist. When someone makes a negative choice, the sinister consequences of that choice do not necessarily fall upon him, or her -- but all too often upon the innocent.

One guide line then is our understanding that if love is to exist, freedom must also exist, because freedom is the only possible soil in which love can grow.

Another guide line is that of mystery. We are trying (with rather limited equipment!) to understand an enormous and immensely complex universe. Plato, Newton, Einstein, Stephen Hawking, Asimov, Aldiss, Stableford, Colin Wilson and Arthur C. Clarke . . . even their great and brilliantly imaginative minds are limited. Compared to the vast ocean of knowledge that has yet to be understood, their far-reaching, pioneering ideas are like palaeolithic men in dugout canoes trying to paddle across the Pacific.

Pain is pain. Suffering and weakness are suffering and weakness. That cannot be denied. Yet for all the reality of pain and suffering, and for all the very real helplessness of paralysis, there is nevertheless a sense in which things are not always entirely what they seem. What we think we are experiencing here and now in this everyday, physical universe may be very, very different from the ultimate, spiritual reality which we cannot yet see.

The writer of the book of Job tried to explain the problem of God and human suffering. At the end of that wonderful and deeply thoughtful book, Job admitted that there were many, many things he did not know and could not understand: yet his faith remained intact.

Our second guide line, therefore, through the problem of pain is to accept with the humility of Job that our inability to understand the paradox of a good, all-loving and all-powerful God in a world of pain and suffering, may well be because we do not have even a tiny fraction of the total data. Like Job, let us go forward in faith, secure in the knowledge that what is incomprehensible now will be revealed to us - in a way that we can understand - in the eternal Kingdom of light and joy which we shall one day share with Christ, Who showed through His compassion and agonising death that God Himself understands all our suffering.

Prayer

God of all strength, courage and fortitude, give us the strength, courage and the fortitude to bear pain as Christ Himself did, to come through it as He did, and at the last to triumph eternally with Him. Amen.

God Himself Suffers with Us

The more we love someone, the more pain and anxiety we ourselves feel when that beloved man, woman or child is ill or injured. We would do anything in our power, including gladly changing places with them, to ease their pain.

Yet the best, the strongest and the truest human love is a poor, pale shadow of the love which God has for us. As the noblest and the most caring human being feels for his or her loved ones, so God is infinitely concerned about our pain and our suffering, our weakness and our distress. When we are sick or injured, and loved ones come to visit us and show their concern by what they say and do to help, we begin to feel better. Their love and sympathy are powerfully therapeutic forces. When we know that those who love us are praying for us, we can feel the comforting power of their prayer shining through our illness and injury. The pain begins to ease, and a little of our strength comes back, when we remind ourselves that the God who made, sustains and loves us really cares about how we feel, that He knows all about the pain that we are going through, that He knows the frustration that comes through weakness and immobility.

God Himself lessens our sufferings by suffering with us, as He did in Christ on Calvary.

Poem

Never alone in pain's bleak darkness,
Never alone in pain's cold silence,
Never alone in pain's deep hunger,
Never alone in pain's consuming fire,
Never alone in pain's relentless presence:
Never alone in pain's tenacious talons.
Our God of courage gives us grace to bear it;
Our God of friendship suffers here beside us;
Our God of rescue gently lifts us from it.
Our God of knowledge shall at last explain it.
Our God of mercy helps us overcome it.
Our God of justice shall bring joy and gladness.

Prayer

God of Gethsemane and Calvary, God of
Pilate's judgement hall and God of the Cross,
God of the martyrs and the persecuted, grant us
Your strength to overcome our pain. We ask it
in the Name of Him who passed through pain
and death to the garden of the Resurrection
Morning, Jesus Christ our Lord. Amen.

Waiting

Waiting is one of the most stressful things there is. Between the taking of a test and the result, there is the awful period of waiting.

It is hard indeed to wait. Christ our Lord waited in the wilderness during the temptations which He conquered. He waited for His people to turn to Him in repentance. He waited in Gethsemane for His enemies to arrest Him. He waited for His Resurrection. Christ, our God incarnate, taught us everything we need to know about life, and one of the most important lessons He has taught us is that of waiting. The disciples learnt it as they waited for the coming of the Holy Spirit at Pentecost. Peter and Paul and the other founders of the Church waited in prison more than once. Holy hermits, and those who have given their lives to the contemplation of the Divine in prayer and the religious life, have all waited for God.

Waiting is part of the problem of sickness and injury. With God's help we can overcome the anxiety of waiting. Everything is in His Hands. We must wait with hope and with patience, with trust and with faith -- and with prayer. We should try to use our waiting time to think, and to plan purposefully and positively ahead. Our Lord Himself taught us to take no thought for the morrow. That doesn't mean we are not to plan - rather we are not to *worry,* but to have perfect trust. We also know that those who wait upon the Lord shall renew their strength and mount up with wings as eagles.

Poem

The seed waits patiently
Within the sheltering soil
Till God calls forth the glory of her flower.

The golden eagle waits
Within her guardian shell
Till God calls forth the splendour of her flight.

The strong and loving adult waits
In childhood's helpless innocence
Till God calls forth her guiding, caring power.

So all of us must wait . . .
With patience for our God . . .
For he renews the strength with which we fight.

Prayer

Lord while we are waiting, help us to
wait upon You. Help us to fill our waiting time
with positive thought, with hope and with
prayer. Let us wait as a granite cliff waits for the
tide; let us wait as thirsty lands wait for rain; let
us wait as the dark, sleeping earth waits for the
sunrise. At the end of all our waiting may we
find You, and the perfect peace and joy which
are Your gifts to us. We ask it in the Name of
Him who always waited perfectly for You, His
Father, Jesus Christ our Lord. Amen.

Hoping

In the story of Pandora and her box of troubles, Hope waited at the bottom. The optimist and the pessimist face exactly the same life situations while facing in completely opposite directions. There is an old proverb which defines an optimist and a pessimist by giving each of them a partly filled glass of water. The pessimist will shake his head sadly and say that it's half empty. The optimist will smile brightly and say it's half full. And yet it is, of course, the same quantity of water in each case.

After some terrible accident or illness which has robbed a patient of a limb, the pessimist will think only of his loss and the difficulties it has caused. The courageous optimist will say: "I've still got one arm left and that works perfectly."

The best kind of optimist is the realistic one who sees through and beyond pain, suffering, discomfort and difficulty, and envisages a future that will shine brightly again on the other side of all the problems. Christ went to suffering and death knowing that on the other side of Calvary lay resurrection joy and eternal glory with His Father and His ransomed people. As we go to our own lesser Calvaries, let us go with Christ and with absolute confidence.

Poem

Hope is the air I breathe, the sights I see,
The holy bell that softly summons me,
To prayer and worship in the heart's own shrine.
Hope is the precious gift of Love Divine,
The Father's gift to each believing soul,
Which makes the wounded spirit strong and whole.
Hope stands arrayed in robes of purest light
That hurl back all the shadows of the night.
Hope conquers chaos and restores control,
Charting the course to joy's eternal goal.
Hope comes as fragrance of the mountain pine.
Of all eternal truths, hope is the sign.
Hope is our proof that better things shall be,
For Hope's clear eyes gaze on Eternity.

Prayer

God of Light, of Joy, and of Eternal Life,
in our deepest and darkest distress, light the
candle of hope in our hearts so that it may
never be extinguished. Give us the true and
perfect faith which tells us that whatever may
befall us here, You are our Father, You love us,
You protect us, and You will bring us at last to
Your Eternal Kingdom where all our hopes shall
be fulfilled a thousand times over. We ask it in
the Name of Christ our Lord. Amen.

Knowing and Not Knowing

God alone is omniscient. God alone has complete, perfect and absolute knowledge. The wisest doctor, the most experienced nurse, the most brilliant medical scientist, cannot *know* with the final and absolute certainty with which God Himself knows.

Tomorrow is a door to which God alone holds the key. Tomorrow is an opaque curtain which can be drawn back only by the hand of God. Tomorrow is an unexplored continent to which God is the only certain guide.

However dark the future may seem by all human standards, the age of miracles is still with us. There *are* spontaneous remissions. There *are* totally inexplicable cures and healings. We must never despair; we must never give up hope. Remember always that the worst that can happen on earth is to leave it -- and in the leaving of it we go to be with the God Who made and loves us beyond our wildest hopes and dreams.

Although the kindest, the most caring and the most honest medical staff, family and friends tell us gently and sensitively what they think and believe about our present medical condition, there is still no absolute certainty about it. Only the Divine Doctor can provide the final truth.

When Christ Himself went to raise Jairus's daughter, there were many who laughed scornfully: yet it was Christ's Divine Power and Knowledge which restored the girl to life. Doubt was also expressed even by the faithful and devoted Martha, when Christ called her brother Lazarus back from the tomb. Perfect knowledge belongs to God alone: ours is a world where knowing and not knowing are often curiously intertwined.

Poem

Within the hermit's cave, the saint's stone cell,
The cloister where the autumn sunlight falls,
Wisdom herself abides with Sister Truth.
Beneath the apple tree where Newton sat,
On the Greek porch where Socrates once taught,
Knowledge and Honesty stand side by side.
Young Cousin Quest relies on those wise hands,
And ventures, fearless, into the unknown.
His God and ours is Lord of every realm --
In His strong, loving hands we are secure.

Prayer

Lord of perfect knowledge and complete wisdom, take pity on us for what we think we know and help us to admit what we do not know. Help us to cope effectively with doubt, fear and uncertainty. No matter how dark the future may seem, help us never to give up hope here on earth and always to look forward with confidence to the perfect and unending joys of Heaven. We ask it in the name of Christ our Lord. Amen.

Helping our Carers

Our Lord Jesus Christ taught us that in as much as we do it unto others we are doing it to Him. Every cup of water, every loving, gentle and encouraging word, every wound that is cleaned, dressed and bandaged . . . All these things done for others are done for Christ. One vitally important task which the sick and injured can still perform for others is to accept with gratitude and cheerfulness those services which are done for them. The word of thanks and appreciation given to the over-worked nurse, doctor or visitor, is a word of gratitude given to Christ Himself. Every courageous effort made to comply with the good -- but difficult -- advice of a physiotherapist, or dietician, is an equally courageous effort to comply with the precepts and teachings of the Lord Himself. Every tiny thing the patient can do for himself, or herself, which saves a carer's time, is something done for God. Because we are currently in a situation where we can do only a very little there is no excuse for doing nothing. God sees and knows every tiny effort that we are able to make. Let us do our best to care for our carers as they do their best to care for us while we are sick or injured.

Poem

Never so helpless that I cannot help
In some small way the friends who care for me:
The gift of gratitude I can bestow.
I will give that -- with love -- to all I see.

The pain may make it hard, but I can smile.
I still can try my best, although I fail
In more than half of what I try to do.
It is the will that counts, and shall prevail.

The will to help, although such help be slight,
Is seen and known by God, and those who care.
The will to give, the will to carry on,
The will to pray for others, and to share.

Most kind and caring Lord, please help them all:
The chaplains and the doctors, nurses, friends,
My loved ones and my family when they call.
Praise God for every helper that He sends.

Prayer

Most loving, caring Lord, Good Shepherd
of the sheep, help us to respond with gratitude
and appreciation to all those who help us in this
our time of need. Help us to do all that we can
to help them, so that together we may
accomplish Your work of healing and
restoration. We ask it in and through the Name
of Christ our Lord. Amen.

Courage and Cheerfulness

It was with courage, cheerfulness and resolution that Christ went into the wilderness to face temptation at the start of His Divine Mission. It was with courage, cheerfulness and resolution that He set His face to go to Jerusalem. It was with courage and resolution that our Lord went to Gethsemane, to the rigged trials before Caiaphas, Pilate and Herod. Cheerfulness, courage and resolution are stout allies: they gallop together to our rescue with the gallantry of the Three Musketeers.

It was with courage, cheerfulness and resolution that Abraham set out from Ur of the Chaldees on his epic journey; with that same courage, cheerfulness and resolution, he rescued his nephew Lot. In that same spirit Moses defied Pharaoh and led his people from slavery in Egypt to their new life. Armed with that same courage, cheerfulness and resolution, Joshua led them to success in battle. This was the spirit in Gideon as he saved his people from the Midianites. It was with courage, cheerfulness and resolution that David accepted Goliath's challenge.

Amos, the great prophet of justice and fairness, strode with this same spirit into northern Israel from his wild Tekoan hills, and with courage and resolution he confronted the people with their sins of greed and injustice and their heartless exploitation of the poor. It was in this same spirit that John the Baptist challenged Herod. This has been the spirit of saints, martyrs and heroes of the church throughout the centuries. It is God-given. It is the spirit which conquers pain and suffering, loneliness and fear. It is the spirit which storms the dark fortress and conquers it. Let us resolve, as Christ's followers, to face whatever we have to face with cheerfulness, courage and resolution.

Prayer

Lord, You inspired Abraham, Moses, Joshua, the Judges and fearless Prophets of old. In Christ Himself, cheerfulness, resolution and courage reached their highest point in the history of the world. Grant to us in our sickness, injury and disability a portion of that same spirit, that we, like Christ our Lord, may come through this ordeal victorious. We ask it in His Name. Amen.

Fortitude

There is a courage which advances fearlessly and attacks all that dares to oppose it: and there is another kind which holds fast and endures. Both are noble. Both are God-given. We may think of them as *active* courage and *passive* courage. A small band of Templars, hurling themselves against a vast Saracen army, is an example of *active* courage. The stubborn stone of a grey-green sea wall on a storm-lashed coast, protecting the village behind it from the fury of the sea, serves as a model of *passive* courage. The wall endures, and, as it endures, it protects.

There are some chronic illnesses and injuries which demand of us that same stubborn endurance. We may face years of incapacity, immobility and chronic pain -- but we must still endure. We go on, and we shall continue to go on. And, most important of all, we shall go on with God.

In my church of St. German's in Cardiff, we are very proud to see those members of the congregation who come to join our worship in spite of their pain and incapacity. They come in the cars of friends, or in wheelchairs -- and by their presence they bring an extra dimension to the service. Their fortitude says: "This is the God we love and serve, and we will not let age, nor infirmity, prevent us from worshipping Him here." They are, by their presence, an inspiration to the rest of us. This is the gift which the sick and injured bring to those that are whole, and we thank them for it.

Poem

It is not for an instant -- nor an hour.
This stretches onward like some boundless sea.
Tomorrow and tomorrow . . . and next year --
Or so it seems:
A darkness without light, a labyrinth
Coiled back upon itself,
A tortuous, torturing path that has no end.
What purpose is there in enduring this?
Lost in this endless sea,
These twisting tunnels
Winding through the dark,
I'll not give in -- I still have God,
And He will grant me faith and fortitude.
I'll not believe in endless misery.
I'll fill my heart and mind
With endless hope.
And if I can no longer move a hand,
I'll still lift up my heart to praise my God.
Christ said: "Sufficient to the day . . ."
And so it is.
I am not called upon to cope with years --
But one day at a time.
With Christ beside me I can win that day.

Prayer

Lord, grant me the passive courage of
fortitude. Make me an old sea wall, a strong
flint tower, a weathered oak that still stands in
the storm, and then, by my example, let me
serve in some small way to show the world that
I still love, praise and worship You. I ask it in
the Name of Christ. Amen.

34

Worry and Anxiety

As if illness and injury were not enough trouble by themselves, they bring with them worry and anxiety. When the breadwinner is ill, there is financial worry. When a carer is ill, there is terrible anxiety about those who were cared for before the illness, or accident, came. When we are ill, we are full of anxiety and worried about our own health and the prospects of recovery. It is only natural that we should be. Yet we worry far more over the health and welfare of those we love than we do about our own.

Jesus taught us two vital things that we must always bear in mind when we are coping with worry, anxiety and stress (especially at a time of illness). Worry, anxiety and stress are counter-productive, and the sooner we can dispose of them, the sooner and the more surely we shall be on the road to recovery and restoration. Our Lord taught us to take no thought for tomorrow. Our concern is with *now;* our concern is with *today;* our concern is to love Him and others *at this instant.* Our job is to serve God and our fellow men as well as we can during *this present time.* Tomorrow is in His hands; there is no need to worry about it.

The second thing He taught us was that perfect love casts out fear. We need to remember how much He loves us, and how much we matter to Him. Whatever may happen on this earth, He will make everything right in the end. As a famous mystic saint once said: " All shall be well, and all shall be well, and all manner of things shall be well!" Her ecstatic words are absolutely, perfectly and literally true. God will make all things well; there is no need to worry on our own behalf, nor on behalf of those we love.

Our task is to love and to serve. That is entirely within our means.

It is God's chosen task to make everything come right for us in the end: and that is entirely within His means.

Prayer

Lord, teach us to live for You, for others, making the most of the moment and of the day. Show us that worry and anxiety are negative and counter-productive, and take them from us. Fill our hearts, minds and spirits with that perfect love which casts out all fear, so that we never forget that we are enfolded in Your everlasting arms, and that no harm can befall us in the end. We ask it in the Name of Christ our Lord. Amen.

Watching and Listening

Alone in a sick room, or in bed in a large ward, watching and listening are often our main preoccupations while we are sick and injured. We watch and listen for the coming of the nurse, the doctor, the friend or family visitor, the chaplain, the physiotherapist, the dietician, the kind lady bringing the tea trolley, or the volunteer with the hospital library books. Since we cannot do very much for ourselves during this time of illness or injury, we reach out with ears and eyes as we might formerly have reached out with our hands, or gone to meet someone.

It is a time when we can watch and listen for God, our loving, healing, Heavenly Father. It gives us opportunities to see and experience God in the healing, caring hands of medical staff and ancillary helpers. It provides us with an opportunity to find God in the caring concern of those who look after us at home. We can listen for God in the loving, comforting, strengthening words of those who come to visit us: family, friends, priest, minister, brothers and sisters from our church or chapel. And we can listen inwardly for the word of God in our minds as He speaks of new strength, of new life, of wholeness and of healing. As we listen we can hear and feel the comfort of God, for it is by His great Name of the Comforter that the Spirit of God is best known.

Poem

I watch and listen as the time wears on.
I see the birds among the rustling leaves.
Grey clouds drift slowly till the sun has gone,
And rain falls gently from the sloping eaves.
I hear Beethoven on my radio,
Watch concerts on the television screen.
Conduct my carers as they come and go:
Life's music has long silences between.
The Saints and Angels watch and listen too.
Help me, like them, to listen, Lord, for You.

Prayer

Lord, help us to fill this time of enforced inactivity by watching for, and listening to, You. Help us to be aware of Your Presence through those who help us, and care for us in Your Name. May we also be aware of Your Presence directly in our spirits, minds and hearts. May we be open to your words and may we make this time of listening and watching a time of learning more about You, a time of true Spiritual development. We ask it in the Name of Christ, Who always watched and listened for Your Words. Amen.

When Things don't seem Real

Shock, not solely in the medical sense but in the psychological one, can have very strange effects. One of the problems that we face in illness and injury is trying to adjust our minds to the changed situation. To wake up in a strange place after a major accident, not being entirely sure what's happened or how we got there, is very disconcerting, and, just as it is vitally important to get the body repaired and functioning properly again, so we have to take similar steps with our minds. These new things often don't seem real. A day or two ago we were living our normal, routine lives: driving a lorry, or a taxi, working in an office, or a shop, ploughing a field, or hauling in the nets of a fishing boat. We were cleaning the home, digging the garden, chatting with good neighbours over the fence: and the next moment everything is unreal and different. There are hospital beds in a long ward, people we don't know, people we've not met. These strangers include the doctors and nurses upon whom we now depend, so the sooner we can adjust and get our mental stocktaking done, the sooner we shall make real progress along the road to recovery.

How can our God and our faith help us to take a fresh hold on reality? Whatever else might have changed, God has not. Whatever else might have changed, the laws of God and the vital truths at the heart of our faith have not altered by one iota. He is still in charge. He is still at the centre of our lives. He is still watching over us. He still hears our prayers. He still accepts our worship and praise. When life is rushing and foaming chaotically around us, and plunging off wildly in directions we cannot understand, the Eternal Rock is steadfast -- and the more tightly we cling to it, the sooner we will regain our proper grip on reality. Our God and Father is the Ultimate Reality.

Prayer

Dear Lord of peace and calm, things are so confusing, so different, and so strange. I find it all so hard to understand. Help me, in all this chaos and confusion and seeming unreality, to keep a firm hold on You. Lord of all wisdom and tranquillity, still the storm for me as you stilled the storm for the first disciples on the Sea of Galilee so long ago. Make my world real and sensible again. I ask it in the Name of Christ, Who was with You when order was first established at the very beginning of all things. Amen.

Lying Awake in the Darkness

There are times when the sun is too bright for comfort. When it is reflecting back from sparkling waves, or from the burning sands of a broad desert, we long for a little shade and some protecting cover from those intense rays. Light is a good, glorious and blessed thing, but sometimes there can be too much even of light.

And at the other extreme there can be too much darkness. A little soft, gentle darkness can be peaceful, restful, calm and healing. Too much darkness can seem to isolate us, to separate us from the sights, the colours, the living movements of the world around us.

Illness and injury often prevent us from sleeping. Pain forces us back to an unwelcome consciousness. We lie alone in the dark, longing for the end of the pain and longing for the light to be restored . . . How can we make the best use of this lonely darkness? We need to remember, first, that the darkness and the light are both alike to God our Father. He is just as close to us, just as caring and just as loving, in the darkness of midnight, or the dim, early hours of the morning, as he is in the brightness of the sunrise, or high noon. No darkness ever obscures God's vision. It was God in the very beginning who uttered the creative command: "Let there be light." And at His command, light came. God sends us a light for the heart and the mind, which is independent of ordinary physical light. Lying awake in the darkness we can still experience that divine illumination inside ourselves with God's help. We can remember sunlight through a stained glass window. We can remember the brightness of the holiday beach, a shaft of moonlight on a lake, or river. And in that remembered light we can find a spiritual light. We can think of Christ teaching by the sea of Galilee with sunlight on the waves behind Him. We can see the light of happiness on the faces of the wedding party at Cana of Galilee, which the Lord blessed by His presence. We can see the light on the faces of the grateful mothers who brought their children to Him to be blessed, and even in the lonely darkness we can feel that same blessing falling upon us. Wherever God is and wherever we think of Him, the darkness is dispelled. The light of Christ and the light of life enter our lives.

Poem

And it is night:
Watches and uniforms, medicine and scissors,
Flowers and teacups hiding in darkness
Like bulbs in winter soil;
Doctors and students, nurses and visitors,
Flannels and brushes hiding like rabbits
In their sponge-bag burrows;
And it is night.
Here in the lonely darkness;
Here in the midnight silence --
Only God and I are still awake.
He is closer to me than the darkness
And nearer than the night.
He is my most loving Father,
My Ultimate Companion.
In the darkness I can sense His presence
And in the silence I can hear our Father's voice
Inside my mind.
Remembering that He is beside me
Turns darkness into light
And silence into the music of Heaven,
Thrilling my soul with His eternal harmony

Prayer

Loving Lord, as I lie awake alone in the darkness, help me to feel Your Presence, to know that I am never alone for You are always here. Let the light of Heaven penetrate this darkness and fill my heart with visions of You and Your eternal Kingdom. I ask it in the name of Christ my Lord, Who is the Light of the World. Amen.

Rounds and Routines

Clocks tick; the medicine trolley comes; doctors and students make their rounds and I am listened to and spoken to. Tests and samples are taken, results obtained, treatment proceeds. Everything is in its place and everything is in order. The healing is as orderly as the universe beyond. Satellites orbit their planets and planets orbit their sun. Electrons in their shells speed round the nucleus. From the smallest to the greatest, there is order. Atoms and stars together share the routine of life and nature. The seasons come and go; there is seed time and harvest. Tides ebb and flow. Water evaporates to fall again as rain, to replenish seas, lakes and oceans. The great wheel turns, powered by the Hand of God, and we are all part of this.

In their own way, the rounds and routines of hospital life are models and miniatures of the routine of the universe, the Divine Cycle. We fit into that routine; we live with it; we move with it. We are carried by it. Routinely and rhythmically, the work of healing goes on. Broken bones knit together again; injured tissues are repaired, steadily replaced by nature's restorative rhythm and routine. Hearts beat, lungs breathe, our blood goes on its rounds and so we are sustained.

Pantoum

Routine meets Order as the clock goes round.
Hour follows hour, and day replaces day.
The seasons paint their portraits on the ground.
The sun's great lighthouse turns its golden ray.

Hour follows hour, and day replaces day.
Doctors and nurses give their healing care.
The sun's great lighthouse turns its golden ray.
Loved ones and friends arrive, their time to share.

Doctors and nurses give their healing care.
The medicine trolley rolls along its track.
Loved ones and friends arrive, their time to share.
Time's pendulum swings forward and then back.

The medicine trolley rolls along its track.
Routine meets Order as the clock goes round.
Time's pendulum swings forward and then back.
The seasons paint their portraits on the ground.

Prayer

Loving and healing God, help us, especially at this time of sickness, to maintain a rhythm of prayer and Bible reading, worship, praise and meditation. May we turn to You at the first light of morning, with the coming of midday and at the setting of the sun. May our rounds and routines ever be centred upon You and may this harmonious rhythm and order bring us new health of mind, body and spirit. We ask it in the Name of Christ our Lord. Amen.

Counselling and Advising

From the earliest Biblical times, God's prophets knew that it was their duty to counsel and advise their people. "Thus saith the Lord" was a challenge to all who heard it. Ezra and Nehemiah called God's people back to rebuild Jerusalem. Amos demanded justice. Hosea called for mercy and forgiveness. John the Baptist demanded preparation and penitence as he announced the coming of One who was mightier than he. Our Lord Himself taught with authority and not as the scribes. God's clarion call was never diluted, never diverted, never deflected to harmonise with "The spirit of the age".

There is too much timidity and uncertainty in 'counselling' today. What is needed is the kind of Biblical counselling which the Prophets gave well and Christ gave perfectly. There was none of this all too familiar "You must think your own way through the situation and then do what you feel is best" nonsense about Biblical counselling. The message was unequivocal: "Repent and believe. Go your way *and sin no more.*" Above all it was our Lord's distillation of all the Law and all the Prophets: "Love the Lord thy God with all thy heart and all thy soul and all thy might . . . and love thy neighbour as thyself." The counsellor who is the true friend of the counselled cannot be 'value-free'. God's truth is value filled and although His judgements overflow with mercy and forgiveness there is no compromise with evil. There is no compromise with sin.

When we are in the privileged position of counselling others we are in a position of massive responsibility. We owe it to them and to ourselves to offer God's truth in God's name. We must give counsel with sensitivity, with gentleness, with compassion, with understanding -- but above all in accordance with God's Holy Law.

Counsellor, when I am sick, or injured, reassure me that sickness, pain and weakness are no part of my loving Father's will for me. Remind me that my God is a God of health, healing and resurrection. Tell me no cruel, stupid, human lie about suffering having some strange purpose, or being in some perverse way good for me. My heavenly Father would not say that, nor would His divine Son who knows far better than most what suffering entails. Tell me also, Counsellor, that miracles of healing still take place. Tell me that if what we call the earthly worst comes to the very worst, my God will gather me to Himself on the other side of Jordan and there I shall live with Him forever in a place of infinite light and joy where there is no more pain and no more death, and where every tear shall be wiped away.

Prayer

Lord of all wisdom, give your counsellors wisdom. May all who speak and all who hear be helped and uplifted by the power of the Holy Spirit. We ask it in the Name of the One Supreme Counsellor, Jesus Christ our Lord. Amen.

Strength and Determination

Those two great qualities, strength and determination, march side by side. They are God-given allies, sent by Him to help His human creatures.

When Bruce of Scotland died it was his greatest wish that his heart should be buried in the Holy Land. He entrusted this task to his loyal and noble friend -- and fellow warrior -- Douglas. Tragically, Douglas and his men, carrying the silver casket to the Holy Land, were ambushed and defeated. With the last of his dying strength, the mighty Douglas flung the precious heart towards Jerusalem and said, "Go on before, brave heart, as you have always done. Your Douglas will follow you as best he may." Strength and determination had done their best. There are some defeats, like Douglas's, which count for more than any victory. Our job, like his, is to fight on with strength and determination: to death or victory. Never give way to despair. Never capitulate to pain or weakness, but fight, fight and fight again. Fight as Christ our Lord fought through and beyond the pain of Calvary to the glory of everlasting life. In sickness and injury we need every last grain of strength and determination. It is a quality which our God rejoices to supply for us, but we must turn to Him in prayer and make our requests known.

Prayer

Lord of all strength and determination, sustainer of the Prophets, Saints and Martyrs, grant me the strength I need now to overcome my present fear, weakness and pain. Grant me the strength of will that overcomes all weakness of the body; grant me that determination of the mind that sees health and healing as its goal and works steadfastly towards it. I ask it in the name of Him whose strength and determination were perfect and unconquerable, Jesus Christ our Lord. Amen.

The Fighting Spirit.

Though all the senses fail and the power of movement has gone, the fighting spirit still remains intact and inviolable. Though pain surges around the body like an angry flood overwhelming a harbour wall, yet the fighting spirit is borne along by that flood -- not destroyed by it. All battles are ultimately battles of the will; the will is given by God and finds its eternal destiny in serving God.

After a stroke, an accident, an operation, or a serious illness, it may be difficult to take the first step from the bed to the chair. It is the fighting spirit which takes that first step, then a second . . . and a third . . . until we are walking again. It is the fighting spirit which gets used to the artificial limb and carries on with an active life again. It is the fighting spirit which says to the sick or injured body -- like some great general inspiring his weary soldiers -- "Re-form! Re-group! Counter attack! Rally! Charge!" This is the spirit that we need and which, if we pray fervently for it, God will supply.

Poem

When life is bleak and dark and cold
And I am weak and sick and old,
More precious far than wealth or gold:
    Grant me a fighting spirit.

When life is empty, blank and drear
And all around lurk doubt and fear,
My God and Comforter draw near:
    Grant me a fighting spirit

When life is rough and hard as stone.
And I must face it all alone,
The future misty and unknown:
    Grant me a fighting spirit.

When life's a desperate battlefield,
Give me the courage not to yield.
Be Thou, O Lord, my strength and shield:
    Grant me a fighting spirit.

Prayer

Lord, you have strengthened every warrior who ever fought for goodness, truth and justice. Inspire us now to fight on undaunted against pain and weakness, weariness and discomfort. We ask it in the Name of our Saviour, Jesus Christ, who overcame all things for our sake. Amen.

Weakness and Debility

It is very frustrating indeed to want to be up and about, to want to be doing all sorts of important, worthwhile and enjoyable things and to be held back by weakness and debility. It is irksome to long to write a letter to our loved ones far away with a hand that is too weak to hold a pen. It is hard to cope with our feelings when we long to sit up brightly in bed to welcome cherished family and friends who have come a long way to visit us, and yet to be unable to do anything but lie back helplessly on the pillows and smile at them faintly. The spirit is more than willing but the flesh is hopelessly weak. God knows exactly how we feel at these moments, and the loved ones and friends who have made such an effort and come so far to visit us also know how we feel.

Prayer

Lord of life and strength and power, help me to overcome this weakness and debility. Grant me patience until it passes; help me to bear it with dignity and fortitude. May those I love who have come to visit me be aware that I am embracing them with my spirit even though I lack the strength to put my arms around them. I ask it in the Name of Him who gave up the power and glory of Heaven to experience the weakness and limitations of earth for our sakes, Jesus Christ our Lord. Amen.

Thankfulness

Even in sickness and injury there is much to be thankful for. Things might have been worse; we look back and thank God for all the good years of health and strength, energy and fitness -- before this illness, or injury, came to cloud our lives. We thank God that there are still things that we can do even in this situation. We thank God for the hope that lives within us, and for the doctors, nurses and other medical staff who care for us so well. We thank God for the families and friends who love us and want so much for us to get well. We thank God for the medical scientists whose skill is there to reinforce and support the work of our own doctors and nurses. We give thanks for those who prepare our medicines, for those who check and maintain the special equipment which doctors, nurses and radiographers use. We thank God for those who built and endowed this hospital.

In workshops and factories somewhere, this bed and its mattress, its sheets, pillow-cases and blankets were made. We thank God for the work of those who made them. So much skill from so many different people has gone into making and maintaining this house of healing. We thank God for them all. We thank You, Lord, for those who built this place, providing healers with a steadfast base. Thank God for every blanket, bed and sheet, and for those skilled workers who made these tiles and laid them here on the floor of the ward. Thank God for surgeons with life-saving skills and for the pharmacists who make our medicines. Thanks for our nurses, cleaners, helpers and cooks. For all who help in any way at all, grant us, O Lord, the gift of gratitude.

Poem

Thank God for time in which to pray.
Thank God for this and every day.
Thank God for each and every way
    In which His love is shown.

Thank God for flowers, trees and birds,
For lambs and fawns and lowing herds,
For loving hearts and loving words,
    In which His love is shown.

Thank God for families and friends,
For healing hands and pain that ends,
For every mercy that He sends,
    In which His love is shown.

Prayer

    Lord, however dark the way may be, whatever the pain, the problems, the anxieties and fears that we now face, help us to look outside ourselves at this time and to express true gratitude to all who are helping us in this hour of need. We ask it in the Name of Christ, who thought always of others before Himself, and always expressed His gratitude. Amen.

Chaplains and Church Visitors

Hospital chaplains and their teams of church visitors are here to help. There is nothing they like more than being asked to visit a particular relative or friend. They rejoice when healing takes place. They care. They are concerned. As a part-time assistant chaplain at Cardiff Royal Infirmary, I recall the enormous happiness I shared with one seriously injured patient and his family when after many weeks of treatment he was well enough to go home restored.

When I first met him he was unconscious in intensive care following a bad car accident. He was suffering from multiple fractures and serious internal injuries. He was not a young man and his family and the medical team were deeply concerned about his prospects. Yet day by day he grew stronger and a watershed was reached when to everyone's delight he was well enough to leave the intensive care unit and go into an ordinary ward.

This splendid, steady progress continued, and when I called one day, I saw that a friend had brought in a portable television for him. His eyes were alight with interest and enthusiasm as he watched the football team he supported playing in a vitally important match.

As I approached he said with twinkling eyes, "Do you have anyone else to visit today?"

"Yes," I replied, "one or two."

"Would you be offended if I asked if you could come back after the match?" he asked.

"Offended?" I said, "I'm thrilled and delighted to see you looking so much better, and taking a healthy interest in your team again." I did the rest of my hospital rounds and came back to him when the match was over. A few days later he was well enough to go home. It was a great occasion.

Chaplains and church visitors to hospitals and nursing homes, and to the sick in their own homes, do their best to share their faith and to help their brothers and sisters who are sick or injured. They do their best to carry out our Lord's injunction: "I was sick . . . and you visited me." Chaplains and church visitors do their best to bring words of encouragement and hope, and the assurance that their sick and injured brothers and sisters are at the forefront of their prayers.

Prayer

Lord of all good works, when we need the comfort of a Christian friend, send us a chaplain or church visitor. Help us to support their work with our prayers as we lie waiting for a visit. Help us at this time of sickness and injury to see in our hospital chaplain, and in our faithful church visitors, a clear indication that You are with us through the work of caring, Christian companions. Bless their work and help and strengthen them as they do it, so that they may in turn help us. We ask it in the name of Him who visited and healed the sick, Jesus Christ our Lord. Amen.

Families and Friends

There is a very real sense in which we suffer more on behalf of those we love who are sick and injured than we ever do for ourselves. It is equally true that the loving concern of our families and friends is a mighty medicine. Knowing that the people who care about us want us to be well again -- and soon -- is a tremendous tonic. Yet when circumstances are such that loved ones cannot be with us as much as they would have wished to be, we are not alone. Christ, our elder Brother and closest Friend, is always there. There are no restricted visiting hours for Him. Because of His infinite love for us, His will for us is freedom from pain and restoration of health. By co-operating to the best of our ability with nurses and doctors, by following carefully the best medical advice, by doing everything within our power to aid the healing process, we are doing the will of God. Every small improvement, every tiny piece of progress, is pleasing to Him. It also brings great joy to the families and friends who love us.

Prayer
Lord, for your sake and for the sake of my family and friends help me to recover, grant me new strength day by day, so that this health problem may be overcome and I may be restored to those who love me and want me with them again. I ask it in the name of Christ who loves us all. Amen.

The World Outside

Although this is a good place, a place of healing, rest and recovery, I miss the outside world. I miss neighbours and friends and the familiar, local shops where I am known. I miss my work; I miss my garden; and I miss my home. I feel that so much is going on there that I want to participate in, and that while I'm here because of this medical problem, I can't be where I want to be, and doing what I want to be doing. I miss my church, my chapel, my Christian fellowship and my Christian meeting place. I miss shared worship with my brothers and sisters in Christ. I miss small, simple things: travelling on a bus, or train, buying a newspaper from the corner shop, having a cup of tea, or coffee, in the little restaurant where I always like to go.

Although the outside world is often a noisy, busy world, I long to be out and about in it again. It is just as much a part of the life that You have given me, Lord, as this quiet, separate world of healing and recovery. You have made us, O Lord, in such a way that we both need and enjoy the active, outside world as well as the quiet, withdrawn, contemplative world. Help us to experience You in both, and to accept with cheerfulness and fortitude whichever world we are in, and to serve You in quietness as well as in activity.

Poem

With the bedside window open
And the curtain blowing free,
I can hear the world You made, Lord,
And it's there I long to be:
Outside.

I can hear the children playing
And the traffic in the street,
Where my bus stops by the corner
Where my friends and I would meet:
Outside.

Give me strength and give me patience,
Give me freedom from this pain.
Old, familiar things are calling.
Father, help me back again:
Outside.

Prayer

O Lord Jesus Christ, You were often at the centre of noisy, busy crowds in the active world of the town, the village or the city. You also drew aside to be alone with Your Father. Help us, Lord, in this quiet world of healing, to serve You through prayer and meditation. Then, when by Your Grace we are restored to our active world again, we shall have fortified our lives so that we can serve You and our brothers and sisters better than before. Amen.

Miracles of Healing

Naaman the Syrian was healed of his leprosy. In his case, God's healing power was channelled through the Prophet Elisha. Our Lord Jesus Christ made the blind see and enabled the deaf to hear. He caused the dumb to speak in God's praise. He helped the lame to walk. Touching the hem of his garment -- in perfect faith -- was enough to cure a chronic haemorrhage. Jesus gave power and mobility to the paralysed. He even recalled the dead to life... and He, Himself, rose from the tomb triumphant and immortal and glorious on the first Easter morning.

Miracles did not end in Biblical times. Christ heals today: in London, Edinburgh, Cardiff, Belfast and Dublin. His power extends from pole to pole -- from the uttermost east to the uttermost west. It fills Africa, Asia, Europe, America -- and all His universe.

Miracles are as independent of time as they are of space. Our eternal God of miracles is the God of yesterday, the God of today and the God of tomorrow. His miracles are not restricted, nor confined, to special nor particular people. They are certainly not limited to those who lived in past centuries. You and I, in our times of need, are just as eligible as Naaman, as blind Bartimaeus, or as the lame man who sat by the Beautiful Gate.

By their very nature, miracles are strange, mysterious and incomprehensible: but they do still happen. There is a recipe for miracles: mix faith, hope and courage in a loving heart, cover with a generous layer of prayer, season with the salt of the earth, then cover gently with the warmth and sympathy of those who care . . . for just as long as it takes.

Poem

The deaf man hears the crystal distant lark.
The lame leap to Olympus and beyond.
Lepers are whole and beautiful once more.
The blind admire the sun on foam-capped waves.
The hungry poor can eat and drink their fill.
Wild seas are tranquil and their storms are calmed.
The mute are eloquent as Celtic bards.
Laughter replaces tears eternally.
The lonely, lost and wandering, are found;
Their wounds are healed; their tiredness is refreshed.
God's Truth -- in miracle -- is perfectly revealed.

Prayer

Lord of the commonplace, the everyday and the miraculous, help us to believe in the Wonderful while surrounded by the Ordinary. Remind us that Your Son, Jesus, was content to live as an ordinary village carpenter, before He called a handful of ordinary Galilean fishermen and saved Your whole wonderful world. Remind us that He lay in an ordinary tomb, before His wonderful resurrection. Teach us that in the ordinary, routine events of hospital life, and home nursing, the wonderful seeds of healing miracles can grow. We ask it in the Name of Him Who performed so many healing miracles, Jesus Christ our Lord. Amen.